GATE Theatre presents

WITNESS

by **Cecilia Parkert**

Translated from the Swedish
by **Kevin Halliwell**

First performed in Britain at The Gate Theatre, London, on 18 July 2002

WITNESS

by **Cecilia Parkert**

translated from the Swedish by **Kevin Halliwell**

Performed by	Tamzin Griffin
Director	Erica Whyman
Designer	Soutra Gilmour
Lighting Designer	Charles Balfour
Sound Director	Michael Oliva
Assistant Director	Claire Bullus
Stage Manager	Lizzy Dudley
Assistant Stage Manager	Kelly Gregory
Set Builder	Simon Plumridge

For the Gate Theatre

Artistic Director	Erica Whyman
Producer	Kester Thompson
General Manager	Daisy Heath
Associate Director	Kate Wild
Associate Producer	James Bellorini
Production Manager	Neil Sutcliffe
Education Officer	Herta Queirazza
Administrator	Maike Mullenders
Box Office	Paul Long

Thanks to our volunteers: Anne Tipton, Jenny Fellows, Ashley Sloan, Lewis Davies, David Linton and all our volunteer crew who often work unsociable and long hours in order that this theatre may survive.

Gate Theatre
11 Pembridge Road
Notting Hill
London
W11 3HQ

Box office:	020 7229 0706
Administration:	020 7229 5387
Fax:	020 7221 6055
E-mail:	gate@gatetheatre.freeserve.co.uk

THE COMPANY

Tamzin Griffin Performer

Theatre credits include: **Shockheaded Peter** also co-creator (Lyric Hammersmith/West Yorkshire Playhouse, Piccadilly and Albery Theatres and world tour, Olivier Award Best Entertainment 2002); **Nothing Lasts Forever** (BAC); **The Fear Show** (ICA); **The Lights Are on But There's Nobody Home** (Royal Court); **Obituary** (ICA and Maubeuge International Festival, France); **Demon Lovers** (British Tour); **House** (Salisbury Playhouse); **Ron Coop's Last Roadshow** (Outdoor Car Opera, Manchester); **Civic Monument** (Serpentine Gallery and tour).

Television and film credits include: **Smack the Pony** (as writer and performer)**; Teletubbies** (as writer and performer); **Roadrunner, Rolf's Animal Hairdressers, Bob and Margaret, Suburban Psycho, The Pay Off, First Sex, The Dream, Great Britain, Medus** and **Kabhi Khushi Kabhie Gham.**

Erica Whyman Director

Erica took over as artistic director of the Gate Theatre in January 2001. She trained at Bristol Old Vic on the Director's Attachment, and with Phillipe Gaulier in Paris. Erica was awarded the John S Cohen Bursary for directors at the Royal National Theatre Studio and English Touring Theatre. Directing credits include: **Silence and Landscape** (NT Studio); **The Gambler** and **Oblomov** (Pleasance, Edinburgh and London); her own adaptation of **To The Lighthouse** (Bloomsbury Theatre); **Blue Remembered Hills** (Bristol Old Vic); **The Little Violin** by Adrian Mitchell (Tricycle Theatre); **Fool For Love** (English Touring Theatre) and **Three Wishes** by Ben Moor (Pleasance, Edinburgh).

As artistic director at Southwark Playhouse she directed **The Glass Slipper**, **The Winter's Tale**, **The Old Curiosity Shop**. For the Gate she has directed **Tear From A Glass Eye, Les Justes**, the devised piece **Box of Bananas** and **Ion.** She most recently directed **The Birthday Party** (Sheffield Crucible) and **The Shadow of a Boy** (Royal National Theatre).

Soutra Gilmour Designer

Theatre credits include: **Antigone** (Citizens Theatre, Glasgow); **Peter Pan** (Tramway, Glasgow); **Macbeth** and **Romeo and Juliet** (touring for English Shakespeare Company); **Fool For Love** (English Touring Theatre); **Forty Years On** (Northcott Theatre, Exeter); **My Mother Said I Never Should** (Derby Playhouse); **The Winter's Tale** (Southwark Playhouse); **Tear From A Glass Eye**, **Les Justes**, **Box of Bananas** and **Ion** (The Gate Theatre); **The Woman Who Swallowed A Pin** (a site specific project at Southwark Playhouse); **Hand In Hand** (Hampstead Theatre); **The Sun Is Shining** (The King's Head Theatre); **The Birthday Party** (Sheffield Crucible) and **The Shadow of a Boy** (Royal National Theatre).

Opera credits include: **La Bohéme** (Opera Ireland Touring); **Don Giovanni** (Royal College of Music); **El Cimarron** (Queen Elizabeth Hall); **Eight Songs For A Mad King** (world tour); **Bathtime** (ENO Studio) and **A Better Place** (ENO, Coliseum).

Film credits include: **Amazing Grace** (Parallax) and **Silent Grace** (Irish Screen).

Charles Balfour Lighting Designer

Charles' credits at The Gate: **Blood of Angels, Salome, The Gentleman from Olmedo, Punishment Without Revenge, Marquis of Keith** and **Turn of the Screw.** Dance includes work with Rambert, Aletta Collins, Rosemary Butcher and Matthew Hawkins.

Recent theatre: **Bon Voyage** (Tabernacle); **Eve** (Kings Head); **Victory Over the Sun** (The Pit); **TakeAway** (Lyric Studio) and **Grace** (Old Red Lion, Birmingham Rep and tour).

Music: **Hagoromo** (Queen Elizabeth Hall); **Thimble Rigging with Scott** (QEH); **3 Bach Cantatas** (Batignano Opera Festival); **Jerwoood Jazz: Solos with Light** (Wapping Project).

Forthcoming work: **Silent Engine** (Pentabus Theatre); **Jordan Town** (with jazz composer Errollyn Wallen) and Richard Alston's new work at Sadlers Wells. For the last seven years he has been resident designer for the Richard Alston Dance Company.

Michael Oliva Score and Sound Design

Michael trained as a biochemist and now teaches composition with electronics at the Royal College of Music.

Scores and sound design for theatre include: **Fool For Love** and **Loves Labours Lost** (English Touring Theatre, RNT Studio); **The Glass Slipper, The Winter's Tale** and **The Old Curiosity Shop** (Southwark Playhouse); **Tear From A Glass Eye, Box of Bananas** and **Ion** (The Gate Theatre); **Knots (in the Dark)** (BAC) and **The Birthday Party** (Sheffield Crucible).

Other credits include: As well as live computer improvisations with Hannah Marshall (Coccyx), concert works include **More Bless'd Than Living Lips**, an opera **Ocean, Chase** and **Hannah's Dream**, a collaboration with the painter Susan Haire, **The Speed Of Metals, Ultramarine, Cyclone** and **Torso**. Michael is currently working on his latest opera **Black And Blue** with Paddy Screech.

Claire Bullus Assistant Director

Claire trained at Bristol Old Vic on the three year acting course. Theatre credits include: **Wuthering Heights** (No. 1 Tour); **Seed of the Bauhinia, Plough of the Stars** (both BOV).

Adapted, co-produced and directed **Miss Julie** (Basement Theatre, Sweden).

For television: **An Unsuitable Job for a Woman, Passion Killers, The Bill and Dangerfield.**

Film credits include: **Conspiracy** and **Cometogether.**

Cecilia Parkert Playwright

Cecilia Parkert was born in Uppsala in 1968 and lives in Stockholm. Her play **Witness** was widely performed in Sweden during the nineties and was recently chosen for inclusion in a collection of the most outstanding Swedish plays of the late 1990s. Cecilia has also written for the Unga Riks youth theatre in Stockholm and translated Rebecca Pritchard's **Fair Game** for the Uppsala Stafteatern in 1999.

Kevin Halliwell Translator

Kevin studied at the Universities of Lancaster and Milan before taking further qualifications and courses in both Italian and Swedish. Besides working as a translator for the European Union for the last eight years, he has been an enthusiastic participant in amateur theatre in Milan and Brussels.

Revelations – The Gate Translation Award

The discovery of hidden riches in international drama has always been at the heart of the Gate's work. To highlight the vital role translators play in this endeavour, we re-launched our Translation Award in October 2001, under the title Revelations.

The response was staggering. The seventy-three entries submitted were of a very high quality and included many plays which have never been produced in this country. Six of the most intriguing and accomplished translations were selected for our shortlist. These were then judged by an independent panel of judges. **Witness** was deemed to be the winning entry, which earned it a full Gate production, and a prize of £2000.

The Gate now intends to establish the Translation Award as a regular biennial event and we look forward to celebrating the skill and significance of the best in translated work in future years.

We would like to thank all the translators and playwrights who submitted entries, and all the sponsors who have made the award and this production possible – especially Oberon Books, Jenny Hall, and the Anglo-Swedish Literary Foundation. We would also like to thank our distinguished panel of judges: Jack Bradley, Dominic Cooke, Jo Ingham, Katherine Mendelsohn, Meredith Oakes, and Nicholas Wright.

The other short-listed translations were:

Death And The Ploughman by Johannes von Saaz, translated from the German by Michael West (***Runner-up***)

Massacre by Bergljót Arnadóttir, translated from the Swedish by Gabriella Berggren

Nirvana by Konstantin Iliev, translated from the Bulgarian by Anna Karabinska

Trio To The End Of Time by Lars Norén, translated by from the Swedish by Kevin Halliwell

Sincerely Yours by Pierre Marivaux, translated from the French by Steve Larkin

The Gate would like to thank Jenny Hall, James Hogan and Oberon Books for making the Gate Translation Award possible, and the Anglo-Swedish Literary Foundation for supporting this production.

Special thanks to the following for all their help and support of this production: Nala, Richard McKane, Rebecca Stone, Eva Gordon, Sally P., Jean-Jaques, Mark Goddard, Penny Black and everyone at Platform, John Garkida, Dr James Marten, Simon Vincenzi, Saskia Reeves, Geraldine Pilgrim, Hannes Flaschberger, Carolyn Roy, Chris Ball, Kate Haldane, Matt Pedder, and all the staff at the Prince Albert.

The Gate's work is supported by: The Jerwood Foundation, The Arts Council of England, Charles Glanville, Jenny Hall, The Paul Hamlyn Foundation and London Arts.

Gatekeepers: Sir Ronald and Lady Cohen, Jenny Hall, Hart Brothers, Oberon Books, Georgia Oetker, The Really Useful Group Ltd, The Really Useful Foundation, and Mr and Mrs Tack.

WITNESS

First published in this translation by Oberon Books Ltd.
(incorporating Absolute Classics)
521 Caledonian Road, London N7 9RH
Tel: 020 7607 3637 / Fax: 020 7607 3629
e-mail: oberon.books@btinternet.com
www.oberonbooks.com

A catalogue record for this book is available from the British
Library.

ISBN: 1 84002 337 6

Printed in Great Britain by Antony Rowe Ltd, Chippenham.

'Man exists but to witness'
Gunnar Ekelöf, *Färjesång,* 1941

Note

The playscript is correct at time of going to press,
but may have changed during rehearsal

Characters

THE INTERPRETER
a woman

Witness (*Vittne*) was first performed on three separate stages contemporaneously at the Backa Teater (Gothenburg City Theatre) on 18 April 1997, with the following cast:

THE INTERPRETER, Maria Fahl, Maria Hedborg, Aida Jerković

Director, Jasenko Selimović

THE INTERPRETER is already sitting on the stage. She dangles her legs while she waits for the audience to be seated. She looks out as if into a mirror.

Is everyone here now? Then maybe I should begin. The question is how.

Why did I write the letter? What a question. How do you answer that? No…there's no straightforward answer to that is there?

I wrote a letter to someone I felt sorry for. Is that so strange? Göran would never be able to understand that. He's been a psychotherapist for twenty years and he still doesn't understand a thing.

I've been interpreting for Göran for nearly three years. It's a long time to be someone else's voice and ears. It's hardly surprising you begin to wish you could act independently. Say something for yourself that comes from within. I wrote a letter to one of the participants. I overstepped the mark as an interpreter. Yes. That's true. When I started here I signed all those papers where it stated quite clearly that there must be no private contact with the participants. That's right, I did.

This guy came on a Tuesday. Tuesdays are always so horribly boring, don't you think?

Can I begin now? Do you want me to begin now...?

Göran and I had just had a coffee break and it was time for a new participant. New ones come all the time so I wasn't especially concerned.

But then he came in.

And he was the ugliest person I've ever seen. Big nose and nostrils like parachutes. Short and stocky, with the smallest mouth you've ever seen. His hair was all over the place. He looked like a little gnome.

Laughs.

Like one of those little trolls, almost.

Anyway, after a while it was time for what he had come for. Göran had asked a few routine questions about his home, family, age and so on. Then he was to talk about what he'd been through in the war.

He started to talk about the forest.

One

He had been taken prisoner and they were going to take him through a big forest together with maybe another hundred prisoners. They walked for miles and miles without knowing where they were going. And all the time the soldiers walked beside them, urging them on. After about fifteen miles he, the guy, was so thirsty he was almost fainting.

Then a soldier pushed a rifle barrel in his mouth.

And the guy says to the therapist:

I thought if I could just manage to nudge the barrel with my tongue he'd shoot through my cheek instead of up through my brain. That would cause a commotion and I'd be able to get away.

Do you see? He's standing there with a gun in his mouth and he thinks he still has a chance!

Laughs.

Bloody crazy. That's what he's like!

I thought it was quite funny but Göran, who always has to be so professional, just carried on with one of his usual follow-up questions:

Why do you think you're a survivor?

Yes, why you? Why have you been given this wonderful gift of life for another God-knows how long? Why are you alive and no-one else?

You have to be quite brave to ask that question, don't you think? I mean…if you've never asked yourself why. Why am *I* alive? They often ask the participants that. Probably because it always comes up sooner or later anyway. As an interpreter I'd never dare to ask that question. Interpreters never say anything of their own accord. You have to cut yourself off. The atrocities don't go right up into your brain, if you see what I mean.

Puts her finger in her mouth, pointing up through her cheek.

It's not me that's asking the questions and it's not me that's talking about the war. I'm just blank. A translation machine.

The guy said he thought it was because he'd saved some of the others. If you help any of the others you get shot immediately. If they find out about it. Like hell he'd survived because he'd helped other people. So damned illogical.

The soldier pulled the rifle barrel out of his mouth in the end. Though he could just as easily have pulled the trigger. They play pop music the whole time. Really crap, thumping stuff.

All the prisoners have to stand up against big grey trees. They're told to bang the backs of their heads against the tree trunks in time to the music. If the rhythm is fast then they have to bang them fast. One man refuses to do what he's told. He's tired and he just can't take any more. He runs out in front of the soldiers shouting that they are just snot-nosed little kids. They are seventeen or eighteen years old and this man is quite a bit older. The whole time they know what he's doing. A quick death is always better than a slow one.

You're just kids and you've no idea how to deal with this sort of thing. Your mothers must have fucked you for you to look so pleased with yourselves now that you've got a bit of power at last. But we won't obey you, you see. We obey them.

Points to the rifles.

Without them you're nothing. Do you understand that you fucking arselicker?

Then one of the soldiers moves forward quietly, takes out a knife and makes a deep cut in his stomach until his intestines start to hang out. At first he just stands there and looks the soldier in the eye. Then he falls forward.

Laughs.

He falls flat on his stomach. I'm sorry. It's nothing to laugh about. I know. I'm sorry.

It takes a while for him to die.

A soldier steps forward and kicks him over, feeling his intestines with his foot. Almost as if he's curious about their texture. First he presses near the wound. Then he presses again on the other side.

And the soldier says: Look! Lava!

Blood is gushing out. Another soldier thinks it looks like fun and steps out to cut an 'X' on some other prisoners' foreheads. But he can't get the blood to spurt as much. Naturally, there's a difference between the abdomen and the frontal lobe.

The soldier, disappointed.

Fuck!

He didn't feel he could say any more just then.

That was handy, because I was quite tired, too. Translating stories like this can be quite gruelling. They get stuck in your throat and it gets…embarrassing. The therapist – Göran – says I'm far too sensitive. You shouldn't take it to heart. But clearly if someone has been through or witnessed this sort of thing…then I can hardly say I don't feel up to listening and translating! You just have to get on with it. It's just a drop of blood and a few knives. Mutilation is the worst. I saw a documentary that showed a picture of a little five-year-old boy making the Victory sign like this with his left hand – the other was just a stump he was waving. He looked so happy.

I promised to try to explain why I wrote the letter. I promised to try to explain. I shall. But I don't know if I'm any good at explaining. It's like when I'm interpreting. I know exactly what I want to say, but it doesn't always come out right. Like I'm not sure whether you understood what I meant about that little boy with the Victory sign and the stump. Victory. Stump.

Shall I tell you a funny story I heard?

A man is about to become a father and he's waiting outside the delivery room. The nurse comes out and he asks:

Can I see my child?

Of course…it's just that I should tell you that he has no arms.

The man thinks for a moment, then says:

It doesn't matter. Could I just see him?

Yes. But I should tell you that he has no legs either.

It doesn't matter, as long as he's healthy. Can I see him now?

Yes, but he has no trunk either.

It doesn't matter. Can I just see my child?

But he has no head either.

He has no head?

No, he's just…a big ear.

It doesn't matter, as long as he's healthy. Can I see my child now?

Of course, but…he's deaf.

Laughs, but stops abruptly.

The strongest people are those who can look at little children's hands that have been chopped off, or eyes that have been poked out or testicles that have been ripped out.

They are the strongest. It would be quite simply absurd for me not to be up to listening, or for you even, just sitting here listening to their story. You don't need to be strong for that!

Eeny meeny miny mo, catch a nigger by his toe…

There was a Greek nymph called Echo. When Hera got angry with her she condemned her to repeat what other people say.

Being an interpreter is a kind of punishment.

Sometimes I wonder why I do it. It was just a coincidence that I started off doing this. When the war broke out in Yugoslavia I felt I had to do something for them. My father comes from the former Yugoslavia, and I'd never really committed myself to anything before.

When the war had been going on for a couple of years I was studying for a twenty point unit in political science at the university. I think it was when I was writing that essay on *Comparative Government and Politics*…yes, that's right, I remember it was a yellow book.

Pause.

It was a fairly heavy exam, worth about four credit points. Yes, that's when I heard about this treatment. They were looking for someone from the former Yugoslavia who could speak the language, but who could also speak perfect Swedish. Someone who could interpret for a Swedish therapist and the participants who'd been through the war. The idea is that the participants come there voluntarily, to get it off their chest. I applied for the job and I got it. But you already know that.

An interpreter doesn't just translate words. You have to get the tone and the nuances across too. It isn't so difficult. You get used to it. In the end you almost become a machine and sometimes I don't even listen to what they're saying. I can be thinking of something completely different.

But obviously as an interpreter, what you don't manage to get across always stays with you. Like scraps of stories that collect at the bottom of your consciousness. Like when you hear your own echo. Less than half of what you shouted comes back. What happens to the rest?

The therapist I interpret for – Göran – is someone I really admire. He's so calm and collected. He listens to the participants and sometimes I just don't know how he can. He just sits there motionless and asks follow-up questions so that the participants can go on with their story. Sometimes they can't go on and he says they don't have to. And sometimes we stop because I'm trying to find the right words so he waits for me.

I really admire Göran.

He sort of has everything in its place.

The only thing I know about him is that he's an ordinary man of about fifty. Divorced and remarried with children from both relationships. He has a house in the suburbs and he feels his work is important and meaningful. Of course. He also has a funny little hobby. He collects tickets. There's an international association where they write to each other and exchange tickets. They might be train or bus tickets, or any kind of ticket. They write to tell each other the exact time of departure, whether there were any delays and whether anything special happened. It seems Göran has quite a lot of tickets and I think he must have some kind of position in the association, be a Member of the Board or something. He's always been the leader type.

Sometimes our thoughts are so irrational. That occurred to me when a woman in therapy told us about the time when lots of women and children were bussed out of their hometown. I suddenly started to think about whether they had any tickets, and whether

Göran was perhaps interested in the journey
for quite another reason. But of course he
wasn't. Of course you don't sit and think
about your hobby when someone is
recounting a traumatic event in their life. The
big things in life are more important than the
little things. It is a therapist's duty to listen to
someone one hundred percent when they're
telling the worst story of their life. I
particularly remember this woman. She was
– is – fairly tall and blond. Pretty.

Two

But she couldn't keep her hands still. She was pulling at something the whole time she was recounting the journey. Suddenly, when they had been driving for a couple of kilometres, they were stopped by a group of soldiers.

When I look out of the window – it was quite dirty – I see that one of the men out there is a neighbour of ours. So I tell my friend who's sitting next to me with my little sister on her knee.

Look – it's him!

She glances quickly out of the window and sees him. She gave me a knowing look that said: yes, you could tell he would join the army. On their side.

We didn't stay on the buses. They dropped us off in a big multi-storey car park. Five hundred people. And while we were sitting in this car park the soldiers stood guard around us. We could have been plucked out at any moment. They had some rooms to one side. It was the guards' quarters I think, and they took the women there one by one. They just pointed out some girl, like this, and she had to go with them. They were standing there with machine guns. When the girls had been in there they would come staggering out.

Do you realise? What they must have been
doing to them in there?

Do you realise? If you had been in that car
park…if you were trying to tell something
like that and you notice that the therapist is
kind of looking away…I wanted to shout:
Are you thinking about your bloody
TICKETS again?!!

But she didn't notice anything. She just
carried on with her story.

My friend and I had managed to lie low and
make ourselves as inconspicuous as possible.
But after two days a man came with a
stocking over his head. You could only make
out his eyes and lips.

He comes up to me and tells me to go with
him to one of these rooms. And I realise of
course that it's my turn now. And the only
thing I can think…is that I have to leave
naturally, because my little sister is standing
there watching and I don't want her to
understand what they're going to do to me.
Nor do I want her to be frightened and try to
come with me. My friend gets hold of her
and pulls her down. I'm grateful for that.
And when…I come into the room my whole
body is shaking. He comes in and locks the
door behind us.

He turns to face me. No, wait a minute…first
he says my name and then he turns round.
That's right. Then he stands there a while
and just looks at me. Then he tells me to
scream, but I don't understand what he
means. So he says it again: 'Scream' and I
try but it's like in a nightmare, you know,
when you can't get a single word to come
out. So he says:

I'm sorry, but otherwise I'm going to have to
hit you.

And so he punches me in the calf and it hurts
so much that I start screaming like mad. And
while I'm screaming he starts to bang hard
with his hands and feet on the walls and the
floor. I don't understand why he's doing that.
But I do know that he's going to jump on me
and rape me at any moment. He keeps me
there in the guards' quarters for two hours,
but we don't say more than perhaps twenty
words to each other. And then he says to me:

Try to crouch down in the dormitory. That
way they're less likely to choose you.

Then he lights a cigarette, takes a few puffs
and gives it to me.

Here.

When I come back out into the car park proper, I whisper to the other women not to be afraid of that soldier.

He won't hurt you.

It was only then that it struck me that it must have been my neighbour. Funny I didn't realise that earlier.

Long pause.

It would of course be absurd if any thought of tickets or timetables should cross Göran's mind. Even so, I find it hard not to believe that it might have done for a fraction of a second.

I tried to talk to him afterwards. Not about the tickets, but about her. About how he thought she felt now, et cetera. Because when I was interpreting for her the tears just came pouring down and I found it hard to get across all the small nuances in what she was saying. She just sat there and looked so small. I just wanted us to stop tormenting her. Not to force her to go over the whole thing once more. Even though I know that that's why she's here. She must be allowed to talk. And I am condemned to repeat. To take her words in my mouth and make them mine.

Looks afraid of something looming up from below.
Realises it was just her imagination.

For a while I tried to decide whether to go
and put my arm around her, but I knew that
that kind of behaviour is not acceptable. I'm
a professional, I have to tell myself.
Professional, competent and strong. So
I asked Göran a few weeks later whether he
thought she seemed okay.

It must have been that day…yes, that's right,
now I remember.

Göran has so many participants and he finds
it difficult to remember everyone's story.
That's only natural. It's not so easy when you
have maybe twenty people a week. Your
mind can only take so much horror. You
have to separate it out. Just imagine if you
were a therapist and you took your work
home with you. You wouldn't be able to
sleep at night and then during the day you'd
be too tired to work or to help anyone. A
professional has to have a shield.

But it was quite a positive story, wasn't it? It
gives us hope that not everyone behaves like
an animal down there.

The day after, she was sitting on the sofa
shaking. It was then that I began to realise
that there was something wrong, I told him.
It was then that I began to realise that after

she had been saved by that guy, something
much worse had happened. She said nothing,
do you remember? Why didn't you ask her
anything Göran?

Sometimes it's better to wait.

But that was exactly when she needed to be
asked!

It was up to me to decide.

Was it? I see.

He hardly remembers her. Memory works
in different ways for different people. With
Göran it seems as if all the stories are pinned
to the notice board of his mind and
sometimes a great big sneeze just blows
them away leaving only the last to be pinned
there. Maybe that's good. I don't know.
Anyway he's a good man. He avoided
tormenting her further.

Something happened in here.

Points to her head.

I find it difficult to sleep, just like them.
Sometimes I start to shake when I hear
certain noises. Sometimes when I look up at
the sky I think something's going to come
crashing down on me. I'm afraid of the
shadows the birds cast on the ground.

Talk, talk, talk, my father used to say. All talk
and not much action.

It's like Göran. He just carries on without
taking in what they say. I've noticed that he's
started to take his tickets to work in his
briefcase. I think he finds it soothing to look
at them. I think he'd be better off learning to
box or something. DOING something.

Three

But the letter. That's right. I have to tell you more about him. He's such a beautiful man… No, not now. He took up jogging when he came to Sweden. He runs all the time now. Day and night. Can't sit still. After that first time when he told us about the transport to the forest it was a while before he came back to the therapy sessions. But one Tuesday he turned up. As soon as he came into the room he said that he'd found a job, a couple of hours a week. He'd had his hair cut, nice and short, and his eyes were shining the brightest of blue. He says he's well. But you can tell that he's saying it out of politeness.

He starts to explain that what he told us last time, about what happened in the forest with the soldiers, wasn't the worst of it. Now he wanted to tell us what happened when they arrived. They came to a camp. He looked away when he said the word. A camp.

The prisoners from the forest, except for the dozen or so that were killed of course, met a long line of old people on their way down to the river. They were being watched over by guards who hit them with the butt-end of their rifles if they didn't stay in line. One used a baseball bat. They were on their way down to relieve themselves.

They all have to do it together while the guards stand and watch. It's more fun watching the old people doing their business because they're so prudish. The guards are about sixteen, seventeen years old. Anyone who pisses in the dormitory has to lick up their own urine. If someone vomits they have to lick that up too.

The dormitories here are six metres wide by seven metres long and about one metre seventy, floor to ceiling. Wait a minute…is that right?

Counts on fingers.

Yes that's right. The walls are made of concrete. Seventy people have to sleep there. But you can't sleep, because you're always on your guard. What's more, you're constantly uncomfortable, lying on top of someone else. The guards have a little game they like to amuse themselves with every night. It goes like this:

When the prisoners hear the guards' footsteps they have fifteen seconds to get up and get into line in order of size, eyes down. If the guards don't think it looks right, they pick out a few they can beat up.

Ip dip dip, my blue ship, sailing on the water, like a cup and saucer O.U.T. spells…

The guards were only nineteen. I'd have a chance to overcome them in battle, but not like this. We might have been neighbours. There were some older men amongst us. My father was there. I'll never forget the fear that burned in his eyes. I think he decided to go mad. Once I saw him sitting there sucking on his thumb in secret. That made me angry and I hit him. He became like a child, turned in on himself and cried a lot. I was furious with him for crying like that so I hit him and hit him and hit him. Once I thought I was going to kill him. I punched him to bits. It was sickening. After all, he was my father. TAKE THAT THUMB OUT! Then the guards came in. They wondered why he was covered in blood and said he should speak when he was spoken to, but he couldn't of course. So I hit him again and shouted at him to SPEAK!

Long pause.

I often think I'm still there in that camp.

Does talking help at all? Some people – Göran for example – think that you only have to verbalise the worst to make it manageable. But there's always something you can't say. It's what keeps us from being easy to understand. It's in here…you can't explain it.

Sees something big and black above her. She's afraid, but clenches her teeth. Maybe we see it too.

Consolingly, whispering to herself.

There's nothing there. It's nothing. Nothing to worry about.

You can't imagine how it feels to be so degraded. I only know how it feels to be slightly embarrassed. All this stuff about having to do your business in public. Once Göran pushed the door open when I was on the toilet. I was just wiping myself when suddenly he was standing there staring. It was so embarrassing. He stood there just a couple of seconds too long. But it was long enough for me to be embarrassed. And that's nothing, of course.

That's right. There was something else about this camp. Everyday the men, about a hundred at a time, had to stand in line, naked. Then a woman would go round with a big machete and point out

– really, I find this hard to believe –

point out which men were to have it cut off. While she was going round looking at them she was talking all the time about what she was going to do to them. Then she would choose about ten of them and cut off their genitals. All the others had to watch while they bled to death. And this guy, he'd had to stand there several times and he'd always managed to get away with it. But once he was standing next to a boy of about fifteen.

The boy was just crying silently, the tears streaming down his face. I tried to console him, and whispered without moving my lips: Take it easy. She won't pick you. Then suddenly she was standing there. And she was about to point at me when she somehow noticed that I seemed to be looking out for the boy in some way so she took him instead. She cut off the boy's genitals and let him bleed to death. He didn't die at once. It took a couple of hours.

And the therapist: Why do you think you're one of the survivors?

Ip dip, my blue ship, sailing on the water, like a cup and saucer O.U.T. spells out you're OUT!

What a fucking question.

Then I wrote the letter. I don't know how I dared. Interpreters have to follow a code of ethics. I know that the most important rule is that you mustn't become involved with the participants or bring them into your private life, and that if you do, you have to tell the therapist so he can use another interpreter.

But I didn't see it as unethical. I just thought he might need a bit of support from somewhere. Then he rang me at work.

Four

He didn't trust Göran, he said. The day after, he came to see me before the session started and asked if we could meet afterwards. He said he'd been glad to receive the letter I wrote him. I don't know why but even then my legs started to shake. It was as if reality had opened up and I'd fallen straight through.

I just wanted to do something. I don't know if you realise how dreadful it is to listen to these horrors all the time without being able to do a thing. Or maybe you do. I don't know.

'Dear friend.' No, wait a minute, that's not what I wrote. 'Hi,' I wrote.

'Hi. I know that you need help and I don't know if I can help you. Your story moved me deeply and I got the impression that you know what it is that you need help with here in Sweden. Is that right? Is there anything I can do? Don't be afraid to ask me. Your fellow citizen.'

When he came into the interpreting room the whole room was filled with him. It was like lighting a candle. It fills the room and smells of church when you put it out.

You want to help me, he said.

Yes.

All the time his eyes avoided me and I never
knew where he was looking. It suddenly
occurred to me that if you stare at a light for
a while and then close your eyes, you can
still see the light for some time afterwards.
I wondered whether it was someone else he
could see now instead of me. Then suddenly
his eyes fixed on me.

Listen, he said to me. You can help me. *Hoću
da mi pomogneš.*

At first it was just bits of things. He got me to
do the shopping and translate the news. He
understood me. We talked a lot about what
it's like when you no longer feel yourself,
and about what the war has done to
humanity. I think you can say that we
understood each other. Even so, there was
always something that wasn't quite right. It
was probably because I couldn't say
anything to Göran about it because it was
strictly forbidden to get involved. At the
same time Göran was increasingly
withdrawn and he seemed to be absent
during the therapy sessions.

Yes, I was attracted to him. And yes, we did
sleep together. I saw it as part of his therapy.
He would often cry afterwards. I enjoyed it.

I was able to touch him. He didn't need to think about that camp anymore. It wasn't their hands he could feel. Just mine.

Then came the day when everything changed.

There had been a muddle at the refugee centre. He was supposed to get a certain sum of money but it was never paid out. So he contacted his welfare officer who promised to get the mistake corrected in his papers, but nothing happened. Since the mistake wasn't corrected he didn't get any money at all, so he got worried and went to the office to try and explain what had happened. There's a female manager there with two female administrators. I'm not there. He told me about this afterwards. Of course, these women at the office couldn't know what he'd been through. Of course they couldn't. But when he tried to explain what had happened with his money no one wanted to understand what he had to say. And they clearly didn't believe him. The more they glance at each other over his head the more he gets afraid. He gets up out of the chair, like this, and says:

There's been a mistake in my papers! No.

There's been a mistake in my papers! No.

There's been a mistake in my papers.

Then the women leave the room. He collapses and a moment later the police come for him. They take him to the psychiatric hospital. They charge him with verbal assault.

That's where he called me from.

When I get there he's just listless. I get furious with the staff and make a big scene:

Why the hell did you bring him here? Do you know what he's been through? What the hell do you think gives you the right to pick on someone who has been beaten so much? And then he screams out and shouts for Göran!

Göran? What business has he here?

A nurse calls Göran. It's the weekend. Then the nurse comes back and says that Göran is on his way. He'd be on his way as soon as he's put his tickets away. The nurse looked puzzled. I didn't feel like explaining. And then came… Göran. And of course he wondered what I was doing there. He took me out into the smoking-room and started to ask a lot of questions.

Are you in love with him?

Attracted to him.

And he with you?

I don't think so.

Why didn't you tell me about it? You know
that as soon as you have a problem with one
of the participants we have to talk about it.
Especially when you start to get personally
involved with someone in particular. You
know that.

You should have replaced me. I felt I had a
duty to get his story across to you. This is all
so difficult. I'm sitting here trying to interpret
for someone who has been through
something dreadful, to get it across to a
therapist and it looks as if you don't
understand. What he's saying really
happened! Are you listening to me? He
comes here to Sweden after living through
such horrors and you can't even be bothered
to listen. Something has to be done about
that. It's my duty to get you to understand.

He moves forward and puts his arm around
me. That's the first time he's done that during
all the time I've worked for him. He holds
me just as you would hold a small child
when it's upset. And then he strokes my
cheek, as if tears had been running down it.
Damned idiot! He still doesn't understand!
It's not me he needs to console.

You should have done something. YOU,
I shout at him. You should have listened to

what that girl who escaped being raped was really trying to say to you. You should have been more involved. This guy was just another case to you. You're so bloody professional that you don't even know who you are. You are just Göran the therapist and Göran the Member of the Board, and you only see what's on the surface. Narcissus who sees his reflection in others without ever seeing what lies beneath.

He just stared out. I wondered whether he could see that blond woman now, crouching down in the car park. With her little sister beside her.

I was as cold as ice. I said: Do you remember Göran? Do you remember…and then I started to rattle them off:

The man who had a piece of his skin flayed off and was forced to pretend to blow his nose in it.

The woman who had to drink her own urine every day.

The guy who was forced to rape his own mother.

Do you remember him Göran? Do you remember how he looked when he told us that Göran? Do you understand how it feels for someone when they tell you that:

They had to bite off their father's genitals and eat them?

Do you understand how it feels when:

A mother is forced to eat her newborn baby? Fried. Fried to a crisp.

STOP STOP STOP. I feel sick! He sits down in an armchair and looks worn-out. I have tortured him. I've enjoyed it. I don't know why.

Like that woman who escaped being raped.

Though she was raped later, of course.

And it was much worse.

It makes for a better story. Not exactly Hollywood is it?

Five

After that weekend we carried on as usual.
The participants told their stories, I
interpreted and Göran listened. But it was
almost as if he was a bit afraid of me. Today
they came in after the session and asked me
to come here. I was to come and explain to
you why I wrote that letter. I know I did
wrong. You're not supposed to get involved.
But even if you forgive me, I'm not sure
I want to stay on interpreting here. I'm not
making a good job of it. I mean, sometimes
I don't want to think about how the war
victims feel, and then I interpret badly,
almost monotonously. It sounds like this:

Monotonous.

'And then he hit me with the rifle and my face
was soaked in my own urine and I was
forced to drink. Drink – they shouted. And
so I drank and vomited, drank and vomited.'

Laughs.

Do you see? Not exactly inspiring is it? A bit
like when you had to read out your own
poems at school and found it a bit
embarrassing.

There must have been a mistake in my
papers!

Lots of people find the therapy sessions helpful. Lots of people work through their experiences and move on. The woman in the car park, for example.

She and the guy I…yes, they bumped into each other outside Göran's office one day. I happened to overhear them as I was just leaving to go to the interpreting room, but I stopped when I heard two people talking in the same language. That was when I finally got to hear what actually happened to her little sister. I thought the girl had been raped instead of her big sister. What she told him was so much worse I can hardly believe it.

You can't take everything in. You'd go mad.

When you're an interpreter, it sometimes feels like you've been stripped of your identity. You're just an echo. In Greece there was a nymph called Echo. Did I say that already? As a punishment Hera condemned her to repeat the previous speaker's words. That is a punishment. *To je kazna. To je kazna. To je kazna…*

Underneath the slime collects.

He listened to her as only someone who really understands can listen. I was never able to listen to him that way. She told him the worst story I've ever heard. That said it all…about the war, humanity, you and me and my darling, darling…I don't know if I feel up to telling you. I'm starting to feel sick. Perhaps you're not up to hearing it either. Her four-year old sister was on her knees…

Long pause.

Ip dip, sky blue.

Who is it? Not you.

Now I can see you're not listening. It's me who can't interpret properly. That's the way it always is. I can't sort of get the important bit across. The empathy. I won't put you through it.

I was only trying to help. To DO something. And the moral is: Don't help out unless it's ethically correct? Is that what you want me to say? That my actions were wrong and selfish? Basically we're all as anonymous as the night and the dark.

I wrote a letter offering compassion. Is that what it's about? You'll never get hold of him now. He told that woman that her story had made him realise what he should do instead of wasting his time in therapy.

I could see them through the crack in the door. They were standing close to each other.

Too close. Then she puts her hand behind his neck and draws her lips to his. I can see he's enjoying it.

Now he's gone. He isn't here and he can bear witness to what we've done. He always used to say that: That was all we could think about, that if any of us managed to survive, they had to tell everyone what had happened.

He told me that, and he wants me to pass it on. To you. To Göran. Though I see Göran hasn't turned up today.

That's enough now. I've served my sentence. After Echo had courted Narcissus for so long without getting him to notice her, she got so upset that in the end she just faded away.

Only her voice remained

remained

remained…

The End.